Life Skills for 6 Year Olds

By Apt Lines

By Apt Lines

TABLE OF CONTENT

Introduction:

Hi there, superstar!

Do you know how amazing you are? That's right, you're already doing so many great things every single day. But guess what? There's always room to learn something new and exciting. That's what this book is all about helping you discover skills that will make life even more awesome and fun!

This book is like a special guide just for you. Inside, you'll find stories, games, and tips to help you with things like being a great friend, staying safe, and even helping at home. You'll learn how to feel confident, try your best, and handle challenges like a pro.

Here's a Little Secret About Learning

Learning something new doesn't always happen all at once. It takes time, effort, and practice. Even the best athletes, artists, and explorers had to start somewhere, just like you. And guess what? Even grown-ups are still learning new skills every day!

When something feels tricky, don't give up. Every time you try, you're getting stronger, braver, and smarter. Before you know it, you'll be saying, "Wow, I'm really good at this!"

Why This Book is Here for You?

Each chapter in this book is like a mini adventure. You'll read about fun situations, try out cool activities, and learn new ways to do your best. You can go at your own pace, one step at a time. And if you're not sure about something, that's okay!

There are lots of grown-ups in your life who care about you and want to help. They've been learning skills for a long time, so they can share tips, answer your questions, and cheer you on as you grow.

Get Ready to Shine!

This is your journey, and you're already off to an amazing start just by picking up this book. So, grab

a cozy spot, take a deep breath, and let's dive into some fun and exciting skills.

Are you ready? Let's go make some magic happen together!

Chapter 1: Growing a Happy and Confident Mind

Hi there, superstar!

Do you know how amazing you are? Yes, YOU! Inside you is a bright, brave, and confident person waiting to shine. This chapter is all about learning how to believe in yourself, even when things feel tricky. We'll discover how to turn "I can't do it" into "I'll try again!" and why mistakes are just stepping stones to something awesome.

Let's dive in together and grow a happy, confident mind that's ready for anything!

What You'll Learn:

1. How to think positively and replace "uh-oh" thoughts with "I can do this!"

2. How to celebrate your amazing strengths and talents.

3. Why mistakes are just part of learning.

A Story About Confidence

Let's meet Alex!

Alex loved to draw. He could draw tall trees, fluffy clouds, and even cool robots! But Alex had a habit, whenever his drawings didn't turn out just right, he'd crumple them up and say, "I'm no good at this!"

One day, Alex's teacher, Ms. Rosa, noticed him throwing away another drawing. She asked, "Alex, why are you tossing all your great ideas?"

"They're not good enough," Alex mumbled

Ms. Rosa smiled and showed him a big frame on the wall where she kept all her artwork. "Do you see this painting?" she said. "I made five mistakes while working on it. But guess what? Each mistake taught me something new."

Alex's eyes widened. "Even you make mistakes?"

"Of course!" Ms. Rosa laughed. "Even the best artists do. Mistakes help us grow."

That night, Alex decided to keep his next drawing, even if it wasn't perfect. He called it his "learning picture." Over time, he realized something amazing—each picture got better, and Alex felt proud of his progress.

Now, Alex doesn't crumple his drawings. Instead, he keeps them to remind himself how much he's improving.

Let's Practice Together:

Activity 1: Grow Your Confidence Tree

1. Grab some paper and draw a big tree with lots of branches but no leaves

2. Cut and put leaf shapes from coloured paper

3. Each day, write or draw something you're proud of on a leaf. It could be:

   - "I'm good at puzzles."

   - "I help my friends."

   - "I can tie my shoes."

4. Add a new leaf every time you discover another amazing thing about yourself.

Your tree will grow just like your confidence!

Activity 2: Say It Out Loud!

Every morning, stand tall like a superhero and say three positive things about yourself:

- "I am brave."

- "I am kind."

- "I can learn new things."

Practice saying these every day, and watch how powerful you feel!

Extra Fun: Confidence Jar

- Find a jar or box and decorate it with stickers or drawings.

- Each day, write down something awesome you did or learned, like:

    - "I tried a new game."

    - "I helped Mom clean the table."

- At the end of the week, open your jar and celebrate your achievements!

Reflection Time:

Take a moment to think:

- What's one thing you've done recently that made you proud?

- How did it feel to keep trying, even when something was hard?

Superpower Badge: Confidence Booster

Congratulations! You've earned your Confidence Booster Badge!
Whenever you practice positive thinking and try again after a mistake, you're growing your confidence superpower.

Tips for Grown-Ups:

- Model Positive Self-Talk: Use phrases like, "I made a mistake, but that's okay, I'll try again."

- Focus on Effort: Instead of saying, "Good job, you're so smart," say, "Wow, you worked so hard on that!"

- End the Day Positively: At bedtime, take turns sharing one thing you're proud of that day.

Wrap-Up Message:

"Confidence isn't about being perfect, it's about believing in yourself and trying your best. Every time you practice, you grow a little stronger inside. Keep going, superstar-you're amazing!"

Chapter 2: When to Speak Up: Tattling vs. Telling

Hey there, superstar!

Have you ever seen someone do something they weren't supposed to, and you wondered if you should tell a grown-up? Or maybe you weren't sure if it was a big deal or not? This chapter is all about knowing when to speak up to help someone and when to let small things go. Learning the difference between tattling and telling will help you make good choices and be a brave helper!

What You'll Learn:

1. How to tell the difference between tattling (to get someone in trouble) and telling (to keep someone safe).

2. Why it's important to use your voice to help others.

3. How to feel confident when speaking up about something important.

A Story About Knowing When to Speak Up:

Let's meet Mia!

Mia loved playing with her toy cars, zooming them across her pretend racetrack on the living room floor. As she carefully maneuvered her fastest car around a tricky curve, she noticed her little brother, Ben, tiptoeing toward the kitchen. Curious, she paused her game and watched. Ben stretched on his toes, grabbed the cookie jar, and sneaked out a big chocolate chip cookie.

Mia's eyes widened. Mom had just said at lunch, "No more cookies today!" Her first thought was to call out, "Mom! Ben's taking a cookie!" But then she remembered what her teacher, Ms. Elena, always said: "Telling is about helping, not getting someone in trouble."

Mia stopped and thought. Was Ben in danger? Was this a safety issue? Not really. She decided to talk to Ben herself instead of tattling.

"Hey, Ben," Mia said, walking over. "Remember, Mom said no more cookies today. If she sees you with that, you might get in trouble."

Ben's face turned red as he looked at the cookie. "Oh... I forgot," he mumbled. He put the cookie back in the jar and turned to Mia. "Thanks for reminding me, Mia."

Mia smiled. "No problem. How about we play cars together instead?"

Ben grinned and joined her, leaving the cookies behind.

Later that day, Mia and Ben were outside with their friend Sarah. They were playing tag in the yard, running and laughing, when Sarah suddenly tripped over a tree root. She fell hard onto the ground and let out a loud cry. Mia ran over and saw Sarah's knee was bleeding.

This time, Mia didn't hesitate. She remembered Ms. Elena's other words: "If someone is hurt or in danger, speaking up is the right thing to do."

Mia turned to Ben. "Stay with Sarah. I'll get Mom!"

She raced inside and called out, "Mom! Sarah fell outside, and her knee is bleeding. She needs help!"

Mom followed Mia outside. She cleaned Sarah's knee, put on a bandage, and gave her a big hug. "Thanks for letting me know, Mia. You did the right thing."

That evening, Mom gave Mia a high-five. "Today, you showed me how brave and thoughtful you are. You knew when to handle things yourself and when to ask for help. That's such an important skill."

Mia felt like a real superhero. She learned that speaking up isn't about tattling, it's about helping when it matters most.

Let's Practice Together:

Activity 1: Tattling vs. Telling Sorting Game

1. Gather two jars or containers. Label one "Tattling" and the other "Telling."

2. Write different situations on slips of paper, like:

   - "A friend didn't put their crayons away."
   - "Someone fell off the swing."
   - "Your sister took an extra cookie."
   - "Someone broke a rule and hurt someone else."

3. Read each scenario aloud and decide together with a grown-up or a friend if it's tattling or telling. Place the slip in the correct jar.

4. Discuss why each answer fits.

Activity 2: Role-Playing Game

1. Ask a grown-up or a friend to act out different scenarios with you.

2. Practice speaking up when it's telling, and staying quiet when it's tattling.

3. Use phrases like:

   ○ "Someone is hurt, and they need help!"

   ○ "That's not a big problem-I can let it go."

Quick Tips for Speaking Up:

1. Ask yourself: "Am I trying to help, or just get someone in trouble?"

2. Remember that telling is important when someone is hurt, in danger, or breaking an important rule.

3. Use kind words and stay calm when you talk to a grown-up.

Reflection Time:

- Can you think of a time when you spoke up to help someone? How did it feel?

- What would you do if you saw someone doing something unsafe?

Superpower Badge: The Brave Helper

Congratulations! You've earned the Brave Helper Badge!

You're a brave helper when you speak up to keep someone safe or solve a big problem. Keep practicing, and your voice will always make a difference!

Tips for Grown-Ups:

1. **Reinforce Safety Rules**: Help your child understand that telling is about keeping everyone safe and solving problems.

   - For example: "If someone gets hurt or is doing something unsafe, always tell an adult."

2. **Model the Difference**: Use real-life examples to explain:

   - Telling: "Your friend is crying and needs help."

   - Tattling: "Your friend didn't clean up their desk."

3. **Encourage Honest Conversations**: Praise your child when they tell for the right reasons and gently guide them if they confuse tattling with helping.

Wrap-Up Message:

"Speaking up is brave when it's to help someone or keep them safe. You can be a helper by knowing the difference between tattling and telling. Remember, your voice matters!"

Chapter 3: Respecting Other's Space

Hey there, superstar!

Have you ever had someone stand too close to you, and it felt uncomfortable? Or maybe someone grabbed your favourite toy without asking? That's because everyone has something called a "personal bubble." It's an invisible space around us that makes us feel safe and comfortable.

This chapter is all about learning how to respect other people's personal bubbles while making sure your own bubble feels safe too. It's a skill that helps you be a kind and thoughtful friend!

What You'll Learn:

1. What a personal bubble is and why it's important.

2. How to ask for permission before touching someone or their things.

3. How respecting space can make everyone feel happy and safe.

Imagine you have a magic bubble around you. It's not too big, not too small, but just right to let you move, play, and feel good. Other people have their own magic bubbles too! Sometimes, people need their bubbles to stay just the way they are, and that's okay.

When you ask before giving a hug, borrowing a toy, or sitting close, you're showing them that you care about their bubble. That's super cool of you!

A Story About Personal Space:

Let's meet Lila!

Lila loved hugs. She hugged her friends when they arrived at school, hugged her teacher when she got a gold star, and hugged her dog, Max, every chance she got. She even hugged the mailman once, though he looked a little surprised.

One sunny morning at school, Lila saw her friend Sam sitting alone by the swings. Excited to see him, she ran over and gave him a big hug from behind. But to her surprise, Sam gently pulled away.

"What's wrong, Sam?" Lila asked, feeling confused.

Sam rubbed his arm and looked at the ground. "I don't feel like hugging today," he said softly. "Can you ask first next time?"

Lila felt a little embarrassed. She hadn't meant to make Sam uncomfortable. She thought everyone loved hugs!

Later that day, during story time, Lila decided to ask her teacher about what happened. "Ms. Harper, why didn't Sam want a hug? Did I do something wrong?"

Ms. Harper smiled kindly. "Oh, Lila, you didn't do anything wrong. But let me tell you a secret, everyone has something called a personal bubble. It's like an invisible space around them that makes them feel safe and comfortable. Some people, like you, love hugs and don't mind when others come into their bubble. But other people, like Sam, might need more space. And that's okay too."

"A personal bubble?" Lila repeated, tilting her head.

"Yes," said Ms. Harper. "It's a way of saying that everyone feels differently about closeness. That's why it's important to ask first. If you ask, 'Would you like a hug?' and someone says yes, then you know it's okay to step into their bubble. If they say no, it's kind to respect their space."

Lila thought about it for a moment. "So... if I ask Sam next time and he says no, that's okay?"

"Exactly!" Ms. Harper said. "When you respect someone's bubble, you're showing them that you care about their feelings. And that's what makes a great friend."

The next day, Lila decided to try it out. When she saw Sam again at the playground, she walked up to him and said, "Hi, Sam! Would you like a hug today?"

Sam smiled. "Not today, but thanks for asking."

Lila grinned back. It felt good to know she had done the right thing.

Later, during recess, Lila saw her friend Maya playing with her favourite sparkly jump rope. Lila wanted to try it out, but instead of grabbing it like she normally might, she paused.

"Maya," Lila asked, "can I borrow your jump rope for one turn?"

Maya's face lit up. "Sure, Lila! Thanks for asking!"

As Lila jumped, she realized something. Respecting someone's bubble wasn't just about hugs—it was about asking permission before touching their things, giving them space when they needed it, and making sure they felt happy and safe.

That afternoon, Lila told Max, her dog, all about what she had learned. Max wagged his tail and gave her a big slobbery lick. Lila laughed and hugged him tight. "Good thing you don't mind hugs, Max!"

From then on, Lila became known as the "Bubble Hero." She always asked before stepping into someone's bubble, and her friends loved her even more for it. Lila realized that being a thoughtful friend didn't just feel good for others—it made her feel good inside too.

Let's Practice Together:

Activity 1: Personal Bubble Fun

1. Grab a hula hoop or use your arms to make a big circle around yourself, this is your bubble!

2. Practice with a grown-up or friend. Take turns asking, "Can I come into your bubble?" If they say yes, step in. If they say no, stay outside the bubble. Now you know their bubble size.

3. Talk about how it feels when someone respects your space versus when they don't.

See? You're already great at respecting personal space!

Activity 2: The "Ask First" Game

1. Think of situations where you might need to ask permission (e.g., borrowing a toy, giving a high-five, or sitting close to someone).

2. Practice saying:

  - ○ "May I borrow this?"

  - ○ "Do you want a hug?"

  - ○ "Is it okay if I sit here?"

3. Make it fun! Act out different scenarios with your grown-up or a friend.

Quick Reminder: Respecting Bubbles Means

1. Asking before hugging or touching.

2. Waiting your turn instead of cutting in line.

3. Giving people room when they need it.

Reflection Time:

- Can you think of a time when someone stepped into your personal bubble? How did it make you feel?

- How do you think your friends feel when you ask before hugging or borrowing their things?

Superpower Badge: Bubble-Respecting Hero

Congratulations! You've earned the Bubble-Respecting Hero Badge!

Every time you ask before stepping into someone's space, you show kindness and respect. That makes you a true superhero of friendship!

Tips for Grown-Ups:

1. **Model Respectful Behaviour:** Use phrases like, "Can I sit here?" or "Would you like a hug?" to show kids how it's done.

2. **Praise Thoughtfulness:** When your child asks for permission or respects someone's space, say, "Great job being thoughtful!"

3. **Explain Different Boundaries:** Teach children how boundaries might differ for family, friends, and strangers.

Wrap-Up Message:

"Respecting personal space is like being a superhero of kindness! When you ask before stepping into someone's bubble, you show them that you care about their feelings. Keep practicing, and you'll be the best bubble-respecting friend around!"

Chapter 4: Learning to Wait: When It's Hard to Wait

Hey there, awesome friend!

Have you ever wanted something so badly that waiting felt impossible, like a yummy snack, your turn on the swing, or for a grown-up to finish talking so they could help you? Waiting can be tough, but here's a secret: learning to wait is like building a superpower called patience!

Patience helps you stay calm and in control, even when things take time. It shows others that you're kind and thoughtful too. Let's explore some fun ways to practice this amazing skill—because guess what? You can totally do it!

The Patience Power Rhyme

"Waiting can be super tough,

But you're strong and brave enough!

Take a breath, count one, two, three,

Patience grows your superpower tree!"

What You'll Learn:

1. Why waiting is important and how it helps everyone take turns and share.

2. Simple tricks to stay calm and have fun while waiting.

3. How patience helps you feel proud of yourself and builds your waiting superpower.

A Story About Patience:

Paul's Cookie Countdown Adventure

Let's meet Paul!

Paul loved cookies more than anything, especially his mom's chocolate chip cookies. One afternoon, the smell of warm cookies filled the kitchen, and Paul's eyes lit up. "Can I have one now?" he asked excitedly, reaching for the tray.

"Not yet," his mom said with a smile. "They're too hot, and you might burn your mouth. Let's wait a few minutes."

Paul frowned. Waiting felt so hard! He sat at the table, staring at the cookies, but it only made him hungrier.

"Why don't we set a timer and find something fun to do while we wait?" his mom suggested.

Paul thought for a moment. "Like what?"

"How about a game?" his mom said. "Let's see who can find the most blue things in the room before the timer goes off!"

Paul grinned. He loved games! As the timer ticked, he raced around the kitchen, pointing to the blue vase, the blue notebook, and even his blue socks. His mom laughed and joined in, finding a blue pen and a blue magnet.

Ding! The timer buzzed. Paul rushed back to the tray, but his mom said, "Hold on! Let's check one first to make sure they've cooled." She broke a cookie in half and smiled. "Perfect. Now they're ready!"

 Paul took a bite and sighed happily. "These are the best cookies ever!" he said. "Waiting made them taste even better!"

From then on, whenever Paul had to wait, whether for cookies, his turn on the swing, or even a surprise gift, he remembered the fun he had with his mom. Waiting wasn't so hard anymore, and it made the reward feel even sweeter.

Let's Practice Together:

Activity 1: The Waiting Game

1. Choose something you need to wait for, like a snack, a toy, or a turn in a game.

2. Set a timer for 2 minutes. While you wait, try these fun ideas:

   - Count how many animals or colours you can spot around the room.

   - Sing a song or hum your favourite tune.

   - Take deep breaths and see how slowly you can count to 20.

3. When the timer is up, give yourself a high-five, you just practiced patience!

Activity 2: Countdown to Fun

1. Use a paper chain or draw a countdown calendar for a big event, like a birthday or holiday.

2. Each day, take off one chain link or cross out a day to see how close you're getting.

Quick Tips for Waiting Like a Pro:

1. Take deep breaths and count slowly.

2. Think about something fun or exciting while you wait.

3. Bring a small toy or book to help you pass the time.

Reflection Time:

- Can you think of a time when you had to wait for something? What helped you stay calm?

- How did you feel when the wait was finally over?

Superpower Badge: Patience Hero!

Congratulations! You've earned the Patience Hero Badge!
Every time you wait calmly and kindly, you're building your patience superpower. Keep practicing, you're already amazing at it!

Draw or cut out a badge with a clock or hourglass to celebrate your new superpower. You've shown that waiting is no match for you!

Tips for Grown-Ups:

1. **Model Patience:** Show your child how you wait calmly during everyday situations, like standing in line or waiting for an appointment.

2. **Praise Small Wins:** Celebrate when your child waits successfully, even for short periods: "You waited so patiently, great job!"

3. **Provide Fun Distractions:** Suggest activities like games, songs, or stories to make waiting easier and gradually increase the time kids practice waiting.

Wrap-Up Message:

"Patience is like a little seed that grows stronger every time you practice. When you wait calmly, you show kindness to others feel proud of yourself. Keep practicing, and waiting will get easier, and even fun!"

Chapter 5: Understanding and Sharing Our Feelings

Hey there, Superstar!

Have you ever felt really happy, or maybe sad, excited, or even a little mad? That's because you have something amazing inside you called emotions! Emotions are like a secret language that help you understand what's happening in your heart and mind. This chapter is all about learning to recognize those feelings, share them with others, and feel better when things get tricky.

When you understand how you're feeling, you can also understand how others feel. That makes you a kindness expert and a better friend! Let's dive into the world of feelings and discover how powerful they really are.

What You'll Learn:

1. How to recognize different feelings inside you.

2. How to talk about your emotions using "I feel..." statements.

3. Why sharing your feelings with others can make you feel understood and cared for.

A Story About Sharing Feelings:

Let's meet Lena!

Lena loved drawing. Her favourite thing to do after school was to sit at her big, sunny desk with her pencils and paper. One afternoon, Lena had a big idea, she was going to draw a picture of her dog, Rusty.

She started with his floppy ears and wagging tail. But no matter how hard she tried, Rusty's face didn't look quite right. Lena frowned and erased it again and again. "Why can't I get this right?" she thought.

Her friend Tom stopped by to see what she was working on. "Wow, that's a cool picture, Lena!" he said.

Lena crossed her arms and pouted. "No, it's not! I'm so frustrated because it's not turning out how I want."

Tom sat next to her. "I feel frustrated sometimes too. Like last week, when I couldn't get the hang of riding my bike. But guess what? It's okay to feel that way, it just means we're learning!"

Lena sighed. "Really?"
"Yeah! Want to try drawing Rusty together?" Tom asked.

Lena smiled a little. "Okay."

Together, they worked on Rusty's face. Tom showed Lena how to draw a big, round nose, and Lena added his fluffy whiskers. By the time they finished, Rusty looked just right.

"Thanks, Tom," Lena said. "I feel better now. Sharing how I felt really helped."

"Anytime," Tom said. "Feelings are easier to handle when you share them!"

Let's Practice Together!

Activity 1: Feelings Faces

1. Draw a big circle and divide it into sections, like a pie.

2. In each section, draw a face showing a different emotion, such as:

   - Happy

   - Sad

   - Angry

   - Excited

   - Scared

3. Whenever you feel one of these emotions, point to the face that matches your feeling.

4. Practice saying:

   - "I feel [emotion] because..."

   - Example: "I feel happy because I get to play with my friend!"

Activity 2: Feeling Charades

1. Write down different feelings (happy, sad, mad, surprised) on small pieces of paper.

2. Take turns drawing a paper and acting out the feeling using only your body and face, no words allowed!

3. Your grown-up or friend guesses what feeling you're showing.

4. Switch roles and guess their feelings!

Quick Ways to Talk About Feelings:

1. Use "I feel..." sentences, like:

   - "I feel excited about my birthday!"

   - "I feel sad because my toy broke."

2. Show your feelings with your face or hands. For example:

   - Smile for happy, pout for sad, or cross your arms for mad.

3. If you feel upset, take a deep breath and share your feelings calmly.

4. Talk about why you feel that way, it helps others understand you better.

Reflection Time:

- What's a time you felt really happy? What made you feel that way?

- How did you feel the last time you shared your feelings with someone?

Superpower Badge: Feelings Expert

Congratulations! You've earned the Feelings Expert Badge!

Every time you share how you're feeling, you're becoming more confident and kinder. Keep practicing, and your superpower will grow stronger every day!

Tips for Grown-Ups:

- **Model Emotional Sharing:** Talk about your feelings with your child. For example, say:

    - "I felt frustrated when the car wouldn't start, but I took a deep breath, and now I feel better."

- **Validate Emotions:** Let your child know it's okay to feel a wide range of emotions. Say things like:

    - "It's okay to feel upset. Everyone feels that way sometimes."

- **Encourage Empathy:** Teach kids to notice others' feelings. For example, ask:

    - "How do you think your friend felt when you gave them a hug?"

Wrap-Up Message:

"Your feelings are like a special language only you can understand. When you share them, it's like giving someone a key to your heart. Keep practicing, and you'll be a feelings expert in no time!"

Chapter 6: Sharing, Taking Turns, and Being Kind

Hi there, awesome friend!

Have you ever played a game with someone and had to wait your turn? Or maybe you shared your favourite toy with a friend? Sharing and taking turns are like little acts of kindness that make everyone feel happy and included. Kindness isn't just about giving things, it's also about showing others you care by being fair and thoughtful.

In this chapter, we'll learn how sharing and kindness can make every moment more fun and help you build stronger friendships. Let's dive in!

What You'll Learn:

1. Why sharing and taking turns are important for making and keeping friends.

2. How being kind makes others feel good, and makes you feel good too!

3. Easy ways to practice sharing and fairness in everyday life.

Imagine This:

You and your best friend both want to play with the same toy. It's a fun and shiny new car that both of you can't wait to race! Instead of grabbing it or arguing, you both decide to share it. You say, "Let's take turns!" Your friend smiles and says, "Okay, you go first!" Now, you both get a chance to play and no one feels left out. That's the magic of sharing and kindness, it makes everything more fun, and everyone feels special!

A Story About Sharing:

Let's meet Liam!

Liam loved his shiny red truck. It was the coolest toy he owned, and he spent hours zooming it across the floor, imagining it was racing through mountains and over bridges. But Liam didn't like to share his truck-ever.

One sunny afternoon, his friend Ava came over to play. Ava saw the red truck and said, "Wow, Liam! That truck is so cool. Can I try it?"
Liam frowned. "No, it's mine," he said, clutching it tightly. Ava's face fell, and she started playing quietly with the blocks instead.

Liam's dad noticed. After Ava left, his dad said, "Liam, how do you think Ava felt when you didn't share your truck?"

Liam shrugged. "I don't know. Maybe sad?"

"That's right," his dad said. "Sharing makes playtime more fun for everyone. It's like spreading happiness, when you share, it doesn't take away your fun; it adds to it!"

The next day, Ava came over again. This time, when she

asked to play with the truck, Liam remembered what his dad said. "Okay, you can have a turn after me," he said. Ava smiled big and said, "Thanks, Liam!"

They ended up playing together, making the truck zoom across a racetrack they built with blocks. Liam realized something amazing, sharing didn't just make Ava happy; it made him happy too.

From that day on, Liam decided that sharing was like a secret trick to make playtime even better.

Let's Practice Together!

Activity 1: Turn-Taking Game

1. **Materials Needed:** A simple board game, dice, or cards.

2. **Instructions:**

- Play a game where you need to take turns, like rolling dice or playing a board game.

- Each time it's your turn, say, "It's my turn now!" and then when it's your partner's turn, say, "Your turn!"

- After playing, talk about how it felt to take turns and share. Did waiting make the game more fun? How did it feel to give your friend a chance to play?

Tip: To make this game extra fun, you can add a "Kindness Challenge" where you give a compliment every time it's the other person's turn. For example, "Nice job on your move!" or "You're really good at this!"

Activity 2: The Kindness Challenge

1. **Materials Needed:** Paper and a pencil to write down kind acts.

2. **Instructions:**

- Write down a list of small kind things you can do for others, like helping clean up, saying "please" and "thank you," or giving someone a compliment.

- o Each day, try to do at least one kind thing for someone, your family, friends, or even pets!

- o After doing something kind, celebrate by saying, "I made someone's day better!" and maybe even draw a little smiley face in your journal to remember how good it felt.

Tip: You can also challenge your friends and family to do their own Kindness Challenges. Each time someone shares a kind act, give them a "Kindness Superstar" sticker!

1. **Materials Needed:** A toy, snack, or item that can be shared with a friend or sibling.

2. **Instructions:**

- o Find something you can share with someone, like a toy, a snack, or even a seat!

- o Before sharing, say something like, "I would like to share this with you because you're my friend."

- o After sharing, ask how the other person feels. Did it make them happy? Did you feel happy to share?

Tip: The more you practice sharing, the easier it becomes. If you find it tricky, start small by sharing things like your crayons or a picture book. Gradually, you'll be sharing bigger things, and feeling even more awesome for it!

Quick Ways to Be Kind Every Day:

1. Offer to share a toy or snack without being asked.

2. Say kind words like, "Great job!" or "Thank you!"

3. Smile and include others when playing games or activities.

4. Help someone who looks like they need a hand, like picking up a dropped toy or opening a door.

Reflection Time:

- Think about a time when someone shared with you. How did it make you feel?

- What's one kind thing you can do for someone today?

Superpower Badge: Sharing Star

Congratulations! You've earned the Sharing Star Badge!

Every time you share, take turns, or show kindness,

you're making the world a brighter place. Keep
practicing your kindness superpower-it's one of the
best there is!

Tips for Grown-Ups:

Model Sharing and Kindness: Show your child how to
share by including them in your activities. For
example:

- ○ "Would you like to help me bake cookies?"

- ○ "Let's share this big slice of cake!"

2. **Praise Acts of Kindness:** When your child
   shares or takes turns, acknowledge it:

   - ○ "That was so thoughtful of you to let your
     friend go first!"

3. **Help With Conflicts:** If sharing feels hard,
   guide them to find a fair solution. Use tools like
   setting a timer for turns or trading toys.

Wrap-Up Message:

"Kindness doesn't just make others feel good, it makes YOU feel amazing too! Whether it's taking turns, sharing, or just saying something kind, your actions have the power to light up someone's day. Keep practicing, and you'll be a kindness expert in no time!"

Chapter 7: Listening and Following Instructions

Hi there, Superstar!

Have you ever been asked to do something and thought, "Wait-what comes next?" Maybe you were playing a game or starting a craft project, but it felt a little tricky because you missed an important step. That's why listening and following instructions is such an awesome superpower!

When you listen carefully, you'll know exactly what to do, and everything will feel easier, and way more fun. Listening also helps you stay safe and be a great teammate. Let's learn how to become a Listening Champion together!

What You'll Learn:

1. How to listen carefully to instructions and follow them.

2. Why listening first makes everything easier and more fun.

3. How to check if you understand what to do.

Imagine This:

You're in a craft class, and the teacher says, "First, glue the paper. Next, sprinkle glitter on it." If you don't listen closely, you might miss a step and end up with glitter everywhere! But when you listen carefully, you'll make a beautiful masterpiece.

That's the magic of listening and following instructions, it helps you enjoy everything from crafts to games and even school projects.

A Story About Listening and Following Instructions:

Let's meet Jack!

Jack was buzzing with excitement. His big sister, Mia, had just brought home a brand-new puzzle game. "Let's play!" Jack shouted, grabbing the box and spilling the pieces onto the table.

"Wait, Jack," Mia said with a smile. "We have to read the instructions first."

Jack rolled his eyes. "Why? I can figure it out myself!"

Mia shrugged. "Okay, let's try your way first."

Jack eagerly grabbed a piece and tried to fit it into the puzzle. It didn't fit. He tried another, then another, but nothing worked. Jack groaned. "Why is this so hard?"

Mia laughed gently. "Let's read the instructions now," she said.

Together, they read the directions aloud. Mia pointed to the first step: "Find all the edge pieces first." Jack nodded and focused. Slowly, the puzzle started to come together.

"Step two: Match pieces with similar colours," Mia read. Jack picked up a piece with blue sky and connected it to another. "It fits!" he shouted.

Piece by piece, they worked together until the puzzle was complete.

"We did it!" Jack cheered.

"See?" Mia said. "Listening and following instructions made it so much easier, and more fun!"

Jack grinned. "Next time, I'll listen first. That was awesome!"

Let's Practice Together!

Activity 1: The "H.E.A.R." Listening Game

The "H.E.A.R." method is a simple way to remember how to listen like a pro:

1. Have eyes on the speaker.

2. Ears open—listen carefully.

3. Avoid interrupting.

4. Repeat back to make sure you understand.

How to Play:

- Play a game like "Simon Says" or take turns giving each other simple instructions, like:

    - "Jump twice."

    - "Spin around."

    - "Touch your toes."

- Practice using the "H.E.A.R." method during the game.

- If you don't understand, ask, "Can you say that again, please?"

- Take turns being the leader and the listener.

Activity 2: Follow-the-Leader Steps

1. A grown-up or friend gives you three instructions, such as:

    - "Clap your hands, hop on one foot, and wave your arms."

2. Follow the steps in the right order.

3. Once you master three steps, try five!

4. Take turns being the leader and making up silly or creative instructions for others to follow.

Quick Tips to Be a Listening Pro:

1. Look at the person talking to you. This helps you focus.

2. Keep your body still and quiet while you listen.

3. Repeat the instructions back to check if you understand. Say, "So I need to jump, then clap, right?"

4. If you don't understand something, ask, "Can you say that again?"

Reflection Time:

- Think about a time when you followed instructions perfectly. How did it feel?

- What's one thing you can do to practice listening better today?

Superpower Badge: Listening Champion

Congratulations! You've earned the Listening Champion Badge!

By listening carefully and following instructions, you're building a superpower that helps you succeed at anything you try. Draw a fun "Listening Expert" sticker to hang on your wall or notebook as a reminder of your superpower.

Tips for Grown-Ups:

1. **Give Clear Instructions:** Break tasks into small, simple steps, like:

   - "First, put your toys in the box. Then, put the books on the shelf."

2. **Use Positive Reinforcement:** Praise good listening:

   - "I noticed you listened carefully and followed all the steps. Great job!"

3. **Make Listening Fun:** Turn it into a game with creative or silly instructions, like:

   - "Pretend to be a frog and hop to the table!"

Wrap-Up Message:

"Listening is like opening a treasure map, it helps you find the right steps to succeed! When you listen carefully, you're already on your way to being a champion at anything you try. Keep practicing, and listening will feel as easy as pie!"

Chapter 8: Speaking Clearly and Kindly

Hi there, Superstar!

Have you ever tried to tell someone something, but they couldn't understand you? Or maybe you were in a hurry and your words came out sounding a little grumpy? That's okay; it happens to everyone! Speaking clearly and kindly is a skill that helps you share your ideas, ask for help, and show kindness all at once.

In this chapter, you'll learn how to use your words like a pro, ensuring others understand you while spreading kindness and respect. Let's dive in and start speaking like the superstar you are!

What You'll Learn:

1. How to speak slowly and clearly so others can understand you.

2. Why using kind words makes conversations happy and helpful.

3. How to practice saying things the right way in different situations.

Imagine This:

You want to ask your teacher if you can borrow the crayons. Instead of rushing and mumbling, "Can-I-have-the-crayons-please?" you take a deep breath and say, "May I please use the crayons?" Your teacher smiles and says, "Of course! Thank you for asking so nicely."

See? Speaking clearly and kindly works wonders. It helps others understand you and shows them how much you care about being polite.

A Story About Kind Words:

Let's meet Leo!

Leo loved playing outside, especially football. One sunny afternoon, he raced down the stairs, ready to kick the ball around in the yard. But as he reached the door, he realized his sneakers were untied. He quickly called out, "Mom! Help me now!"

His mom turned around; her eyebrows raised. "Leo," she said gently, "when you need something, it's important to ask kindly. It makes people want to help you."

Leo frowned. He didn't mean to sound bossy; he just wanted to play as soon as possible! He took a deep breath, trying to remember what his mom had said before. "Mom, could you please help me tie my shoes?"

His mom smiled. "Of course, Leo! That was much nicer."

As she tied his laces, Leo noticed how her smile made him feel better too. "Thank you!" he said when she finished.

Later that day, Leo was playing football with his friend Sophie. During the game, he kicked the ball out of bounds and accidentally hit a flower pot near the fence. "Leo!" Sophie said. "You need to be more careful!"

Leo remembered what his mom had said about kind words. Instead of getting upset, he said, "I'm sorry, Sophie. I'll be more careful. Do you want to help me fix the flowers?"

Sophie's frown turned into a grin. "Sure!" she said, picking up the pot with Leo.

By the end of the day, Leo felt proud. He realized that kind words didn't just make other people happy; they made everything easier and more fun too. From then on, he tried to use kind words whenever he needed help, had to apologize, or wanted to share something.

Let's Practice Together!

Activity 1: Say It Kindly Game

1. Think of common things you might ask for, like a snack, help with homework, or a toy.

2. Practice asking in a kind and clear way. Use "please" when you ask and "thank you" when you receive something.

   - For example:

     - "Could you help me with my puzzle, please?"

     - "May I have a snack, please?"

     - "Thank you for helping me!"

3. Take turns practicing with a grown-up or friend, and give each other compliments when you ask politely.

Challenge: Try this game during real situations, like at dinner or when playing. Notice how people respond when you use kind words!

Activity 2: Tongue Twister Challenge

1. Practice speaking clearly with these fun tongue twisters:

   - "She sells seashells by the seashore."

- ○ "Red lorry, yellow lorry."
  - ○ "How much wood would a woodchuck chuck if a woodchuck could chuck wood?"

2. Start slow and make sure to pronounce each word clearly.

3. Once you feel confident, speed it up and see how fast you can go without making a mistake!

Bonus Challenge: Make up your own tongue twisters with silly words or phrases like, "Silly snakes slither slowly" or "Bouncing bunnies baked bread."

Quick Tips to Speak Like a Pro:

1. **Take a deep breath**: Before you start talking, take a moment to relax so your words don't come out too fast.

2. **Look at the person you're speaking to**: This shows you're being thoughtful and helps them focus on what you're saying.

3. **Use kind words**: Say "please," "thank you," "excuse me," and "you're welcome" whenever you can.

4. **Check if the person understood you**: Ask, "Did that make sense?" or "Do you need me to explain more?"

Reflection Time:

- Can you remember a time when you used kind words? How did it make you feel?

- What's one kind thing you could say to someone today?

Superpower Badge: Kind Communicator

Congratulations! You've earned the Kind Communicator Badge!
Every time you speak clearly and kindly, you're making conversations more fun and meaningful. Draw a speech bubble with a smiley face in it, or make a "Kind Words Champion" sticker to remind yourself of your superpower!

Tips for Grown-Ups:

1. **Model Clear and Kind Communication:** Speak slowly, pronounce words clearly, and use polite phrases like "please" and "thank you." Your child will follow your example!

2. **Praise Kindness:** When your child speaks kindly or asks politely, say something like:

- o "That was so thoughtful of you to say 'please.' Great job!"

- o "I really liked how you asked so nicely."

3. **Make It Fun**: Play games like "Polite Conversation Bingo," where kids check off polite phrases they use during the day, or practice silly tongue twisters together to build confidence.

Wrap-Up Message:

"Your words have the power to make someone smile, feel good, or understand you better. When you speak clearly and kindly, you're showing the world how thoughtful and amazing you are.

Each word you choose carefully helps your friendships grow stronger, makes others happy, and shows how thoughtful and amazing you are. Keep practicing, and soon it will feel as natural as a sunny day!"

Chapter 9: Exploring the World Around You

Hey there, little explorer!

Have you ever looked up at the stars and wondered how far away they are? Or watched a butterfly flutter by and thought, "Where does it go when it flies away?" That's your amazing curiosity at work. It's like a superpower that helps you discover new things about the world around you.

This chapter will show you how to explore, ask exciting questions, and turn every day into an adventure. Let's put on our explorer hats and dive into the wonders of our amazing world!

What You'll Learn:

1. How to use your curiosity to explore new things.

2. How to ask questions that help you learn and grow.

3. How to turn curiosity into a superpower for discovering new things.

Imagine This:

You're walking in the park and see a little bug crawling on a leaf. Instead of walking by, you stop and ask, "What kind of bug is this? Where is it going?" You find a grown-up to help you look it up, and together, you learn that it's a ladybug searching for food.

Now you know something new, all because you stopped to explore. See? Your curiosity just turned a simple walk into a big discovery!

A Story About Curiosity:

Let's meet Nora!

Nora loved collecting rocks. She had a big jar filled with rocks of all colours and shapes that she found in her backyard, at the beach, or on walks with her dad. One sunny afternoon, Nora saw a shiny, colourful rock glinting by the river. She picked it up and turned it over in her hand. It sparkled in the sunlight. "What kind of rock is this?" she wondered.

"Dad!" she called. "Do you know what kind of rock this is?"

Her dad looked at the rock and shook his head. "I'm not sure, Nora. But let's find out together."

They walked to the library and found a big book about rocks and minerals. Nora flipped through the pages until she found a picture of a rock that looked just like hers. "It's a geode!" she exclaimed. "It says there could be crystals inside!"

Her dad smiled. "Wow, Nora! You're like a real scientist, making discoveries."

Excited, Nora couldn't wait to learn more. She

borrowed the book, brought it home, and spent the evening reading all about rocks. She even wrote down her favourite facts in her explorer notebook.

Nora felt proud of her discovery and couldn't wait to go exploring again. From that day on, she knew her curiosity was her superpower!

Let's Practice Together!

Activity 1: Nature Scavenger Hunt

Materials Needed:

- A notebook or piece of paper

- A pencil or crayons

Instructions:

1. Go outside with a grown-up and look for interesting things in nature. Here's a checklist to get you started:

      ○ A flower in a colour you've never noticed.

      ○ Something that moves, like an ant, bird, or squirrel.

      ○ A rock with a cool shape or a leaf with a unique pattern.

2. For each item you find, stop, and ask a question, like:

      ○ "Why do flowers grow in different colours?"

      ○ "Where does the squirrel go at night?"

3. Draw or write about your discoveries in your notebook.

4. Share your findings with someone at home!

Activity 2: Ask a "Why" Question

Materials Needed:

- A notebook or paper

- A grown-up or book to help you find answers

Instructions:

1. Think of something you see every day, like the sun, clouds, or trees.

2. Ask a question about it, like:

      ○ "Why is the sky blue?"

- ○ "How do trees grow so tall?"
- ○ "What makes a rainbow?"

3. Write down your question and search for the answer using a book, the internet (with a grown-up's help), or by asking someone who knows.

4. Draw a picture of what you learned to help you remember!

Quick Tips for Little Explorers:

1. Always stop and ask, "What is that?" or "Why does that happen?"

2. Keep a notebook to draw or write about cool things you see.

3. Don't be afraid to ask for help when you're curious about something!

4. Share your discoveries with friends and family, it makes exploring even more fun!

Reflection Time:

- What's the coolest thing you've ever discovered? How did you find out about it?

- What's one thing you're curious about today?

Superpower Badge: Discovery Dynamo

Congratulations! You've earned the Discovery Dynamo Badge!
Every time you ask a question or learn something new, you're unlocking the secrets of the world around you. Draw a badge with a magnifying glass or a globe to remind yourself that you're an incredible explorer!

Tips for Grown-Ups:

1. **Encourage Questions:** When your child asks "why," take the time to answer or explore the answer together.

2. **Model Curiosity:** Share your own questions, like, "I wonder why leaves change colours in the fall?" or "Let's find out where clouds come from."

3. **Provide Tools for Exploring:** Give your child a magnifying glass, maps, or books to fuel their curiosity.

4. **Celebrate Discoveries:** Praise them for asking questions and finding answers: "That's a great question!" or "Wow, I didn't know that. Thanks for teaching me!"

Wrap-Up Message:

"The world is full of amazing things waiting for you to explore. Every question you ask is like a key that opens a door to something new. Keep wondering, asking, and discovering. You're already an incredible little explorer!"

Chapter 10: Asking for Help When You Need It

Hi there, Superstar!

Do you ever get stuck trying to do something and feel unsure what to do next? Maybe your shoelace won't tie, you're struggling with a tricky puzzle, or you can't reach something on a high shelf. Guess what? It's *always* okay to ask for help!

Even grown-ups ask for help when they need it. Asking for help is smart, brave, and it helps you learn new things. This chapter will show you how asking for help can make life easier, safer, and even more fun. Let's explore your "Help Superpower" together!

The Help Superpower Rhyme

When you're stuck and don't know what to do,

Ask for help, and it's good for you!

"Please" and "thank you," say them with care,

Someone will help you, always fair!

What You'll Learn:

1. Why asking for help is a good thing.

2. How to ask for help politely and clearly.

3. How to decide when to try on your own and when to ask for help.

Imagine This:

You're trying to solve a hard puzzle. You try turning the pieces every which way, but nothing seems to fit. Instead of giving up, you ask your friend, "Can you help me figure this out?" Your friend shows you a trick to find the corner pieces first, and together, you solve it in no time.

See? Asking for help isn't just smart. It makes hard things easier and more fun!

A Story About Asking for Help:

Let's meet Chloe!

Chloe loved watching her big brother zoom around the yard on his bike. She wanted to ride her bike without training wheels too. "If he can do it, I can do it!" she thought.

One sunny afternoon, Chloe decided to try. She wobbled as she pedalled, and boom! She fell onto the grass. "Ouch!" Chloe said, brushing herself off. She tried again and again, but every time, she wobbled and fell.

Frustrated, Chloe sat down on the porch. "Why can't I get this?" she wondered.

Her dad came outside and sat next to her. "What's wrong, Chloe?"

"I can't ride my bike without training wheels, and I keep falling!" she said, tears in her eyes.

Her dad smiled gently. "It's okay to need a little help when you're learning something new. Even your brother needed help when he started."

Chloe sniffled. "Really?" "Really," her dad said. "How about I hold the bike while you pedal?"

 Chloe nodded. Her dad steadied the bike as she climbed on. Slowly, she began to pedal. "You're doing it!" her dad said, letting go for a moment. Chloe wobbled but kept going.

By the end of the afternoon, Chloe was riding her bike all by herself. She grinned from ear to ear. "Thanks for helping me, Dad!"

Her dad hugged her. "Asking for help doesn't make you weaker, Chloe. It makes you stronger and braver."

From that day on, Chloe knew that asking for help was a superpower that helped her grow!

Let's Practice Together!

Activity 1: The Help Challenge

Materials Needed: A grown-up or friend to help.

Instructions:

1. Think of situations where you might need help, like:

    - Reaching a high shelf.

    - Tying your shoes.

    - Carrying something heavy.

2. Practice asking for help using polite phrases like:

    - "Can you help me with this, please?"

    - "I'm having trouble. Could you show me how to do it?"

3. After receiving help, always say, "Thank you!"

4. Talk about how it feels to ask for and receive help.

Activity 2: Help or try?

Materials Needed: A grown-up or friend to give examples.

Instructions:
Have the grown-up or friend describe different situations, like:

- "You need to open a jar that's too tight."
- "You're trying to draw a tricky picture."
- "You're trying to figure out a hard math problem."

2. Decide if it's something you can try on your own or if you should ask for help.

3. Discuss your choices. Why did you decide to ask for help or try it yourself?

Quick Tips for Asking for Help:

1. Use polite words like "please" and "thank you."

2. Look at the person you're asking. It shows you're serious and respectful.

3. Don't be afraid to ask. Everyone needs help sometimes!

4. Practice helping others too. It's a great way to build teamwork.

Reflection Time:

- Think about a time when you asked for help. How did it feel?

- Can you think of something you might need help with today?

Superpower Badge: Help Hero

Congratulations! You've earned the Help Hero Badge!
Every time you ask for help, you're growing stronger and braver. Draw a badge with a hand reaching out to help someone, or make a "Helping Superstar" sticker to remind yourself of your superpower!

Tips for Grown-Ups:

1. **Encourage Asking:** Let your child know that asking for help is a strength, not a weakness. Praise them when they ask, like:

   - "I'm so glad you asked for help. That was such a smart thing to do!"

2. **Model Asking for Help:** Show your child how you ask for help, like saying:

   - "Could you hold the door for me, please?" or "I can't reach that. Can you help me?"

3. **Balance Independence**: Help your child decide
   when to try something on their own and when
   it's okay to ask for help.

Wrap-Up Message:

"Asking for help doesn't mean you're not strong. It means you're smart! When you ask for help, you learn something new, stay safe, and grow even stronger. Keep practicing, and you'll always know when to try on your own and when to ask for a hand!"

Chapter 11: Helping at Home

Hello, Fantastic Helper!

Do you know what's super cool about being part of a family or a team? Everyone helps out! Whether it's setting the table, tidying up toys, or feeding a pet, helping at home isn't just about chores—it's about kindness, responsibility, and teamwork.

In this chapter, you'll learn fun and simple ways to be a Helping Hero and discover why your small actions can make a BIG difference. Let's roll up our sleeves and get started!

What You'll Learn:

1. Why helping at home is important and how it shows kindness and responsibility.

2. Fun and simple ways to help around the house.

3. How teamwork makes your family stronger and happier.

Imagine This:

You notice the table is messy after lunch. Instead of waiting for someone else to clean it, you grab a cloth and wipe it down. Your grown-up smiles and says, "Thank you! That was so thoughtful."

Now the table is clean, your grown-up is happy, and you feel proud of yourself. Way to go, Helping Hero!

A Story About Helping:

Let's meet Finn!

Finn was playing with his toys when he noticed his mom outside carrying grocery bags. Her arms were full, and she was trying to open the door with her elbow.

Finn paused. He remembered his teacher saying, "Even small acts of kindness make a big difference." He jumped up and ran to the door. "I'll help, Mom!" he said, opening it wide.

His mom smiled. "Thank you, Finn! That was such a big help."

Finn felt proud. Helping felt so good that he started noticing other ways he could pitch in.

Later, he saw his dog's empty food bowl. "I can do this!" he said, pouring food into the bowl carefully. The dog wagged its tail, and Finn laughed.

That evening, Finn's dad came home and looked tired. Finn thought, "What can I do to help him?" He ran to grab his dad's shoes and put them away. His dad smiled

and said, "Thanks, buddy. That was so thoughtful."

Finn realized that helping wasn't just about chores. It was about showing love to his family. Each time he helped, his family felt happier, and so did he.

And that made him feel like a real superhero!

Let's Practice Together!

Activity 1: Chore Bingo

Materials Needed: A piece of paper, a ruler, and markers or stickers.

Instructions:

1. Create a bingo card with simple chores in each box, like:

   - Make your bed.

   - Set the table.

   - Pick up toys.

   - Water the plants.

   - Feed the pet.

2. Each time you complete a chore, mark off the box with a sticker or checkmark.

3. When you get a bingo (a full row, column, or diagonal), celebrate with a high-five, a small reward, or a family cheer!

Activity 2: Helping Hands Jar

Materials Needed: A jar, paper, and scissors.

Instructions:

1. Write small chores or helpful actions on slips of paper, such as:

    ○ Sweep the floor.

    ○ Put away the dishes.

    ○ Help fold the laundry.

    ○ Clear the table after a meal.

2. Fold the slips of paper and put them in the jar.

3. Each day, pick one slip from the jar and complete the task.

4. Add new ideas to the jar whenever you think of more ways to help.

Quick Ways to Be a Helping Hero:

1. Ask, "What can I do to help?" whenever you see someone busy.

2. Clean up your toys or books as soon as you're done playing.

3. Do one surprise chore each week, like watering the plants or setting the table without being asked.

Reflection Time:

- What's one chore or task you enjoy doing to help out?

- How does it feel when someone thanks you for helping?

- What's one new way you can help your family this week?

Superpower Badge: Helping Hero

Congratulations! You've earned the Helping Hero Badge!
Helping at home makes you responsible, thoughtful, and kind. Draw a badge with a broom, a toy box, or a big smile to remind yourself that you're making your home a happier place every day!

Tips for Grown-Ups:

1. **Make It Fun**: Turn chores into games or challenges, like "Let's see who can clean up the fastest!"

2. **Show Appreciation**: Always thank your child for helping out, even with small tasks. Saying, "That really helped!" or "You made my day easier!" reinforces good habits.

3. **Start Small**: Give age-appropriate tasks, like wiping surfaces or putting away toys, to build your child's confidence.

Wrap-Up Message:

"Helping at home isn't just about cleaning. It's about caring for the people you love. Every time you lend a hand, you're making your home a happier place. Keep being awesome, and watch how your family smiles when you help. You're a true Helping Hero!"

Chapter 12: Staying Safe and Smart

Hi there, Smart Friend!

Do you know what makes a real superhero? It's not just about super strength or cool gadgets. It's about staying safe and making smart choices every day. Whether you're at home, outside playing, or crossing the street, there are simple rules to follow that help keep you and others safe. This chapter will teach you how to use your **safety superpowers** to be a true hero in every situation. Let's get started!

What You'll Learn:

1. Basic safety rules for home, school, and play.

2. How to stay aware of your surroundings and avoid danger.

3. The importance of listening to trusted adults about safety.

Imagine This:

You're walking to the park with your friend, and you need to cross the street. You stop at the curb and remember the safety steps your grown-up taught you: "Stop, look both ways, and listen for cars." You wait until the street is completely clear, then walk across safely.

Your friend says, "Wow, you're really good at staying safe!" That's because you used your safety superpowers. Great job!

A Story About Safety:

Let's meet Amara!

Amara loved riding her shiny blue scooter. She would zoom around the neighbourhood, pretending she was a superhero racing to save the day. But one afternoon, as she hurried outside, she forgot to put on her helmet.

Her dad saw her and called out, "Amara, where's your helmet?"

Amara shrugged. "I don't need it. I'm just riding on the

sidewalk."

Her dad knelt down next to her. "Even superheroes wear helmets to protect their heads. Your helmet is like your superhero shield—it keeps you safe no matter what."

Amara thought about it. "Really? Even superheroes?"

Her dad smiled. "Absolutely! And you're a superhero when you choose to stay safe."

Amara grabbed her helmet and buckled it on. She felt ready to zoom, knowing she was protected. As she rode her scooter, she noticed a big crack in the sidewalk ahead and steered around it. "Good thing I'm being careful!" she thought.

From that day on, Amara always wore her helmet and followed safety rules. She knew that being safe wasn't just smart. It was cool!

Let's Practice Together!

Activity 1: The Safety Game

Materials Needed: Paper and markers or crayons.

Instructions:

1. Think about places where safety rules are important, like:

    - At home (e.g., don't touch hot stoves or sharp objects).

- On the road (e.g., always look both ways before crossing the street).
- On the playground (e.g., wait your turn on the slide).

2. Create a list of "Safety Do's" and "Safety Don'ts" for each place.

- Example:
  - **Safety Do**: Wear a helmet when riding a bike.
  - **Safety Don't**: Run into the street without looking.

3. Draw pictures for each rule to make your list fun and colourful!

Activity 2: Safety Quiz

Materials Needed: A grown-up to ask questions.

Instructions:

1. A grown-up can ask safety questions like:
   - "What do you do if you see a stranger?"
   - "How do you cross the street safely?"
   - "Why should you wear a helmet on your bike or scooter?"

2. Answer the questions and earn points for each correct answer.

3. When you score enough points, celebrate by creating a "Safety Hero Certificate" for yourself!

Quick Safety Tips for Superstars:

1. Always tell a grown-up where you're going before you leave.

2. Never talk to strangers or go anywhere without a trusted adult.

3. Stop, look both ways, and listen for cars before crossing the street.

4. Always wear safety gear, like helmets and seat belts.

Reflection Time:

- Can you think of a time when you stayed safe by following a rule?

- What's one new safety rule you learned today that you'll remember?

Superpower Badge: Safety Hero

Congratulations! You've earned the Safety Hero Badge!

Every time you follow a safety rule, you're protecting yourself and others. Draw a badge with a shield or a traffic light to remind yourself that being safe is smart and cool!

Tips for Grown-Ups:

1. **Teach by Example:** Model safety habits like wearing seat belts, crossing streets carefully, and staying alert. Kids learn by watching you!

2. **Use Simple Language:** Explain rules clearly, like "Hot things can burn you, so don't touch."

3. **Make It Fun:** Turn safety lessons into games, like pretending to be superheroes following their mission rules.

4. **Praise Smart Choices:** When your child follows a safety rule, say, "Great job staying safe! That was so smart of you."

Wrap-Up Message:

"Being safe doesn't mean you're scared. It means you're smart! Every time you follow safety rules, you're taking care of yourself and the people around you. Keep practicing, and you'll always be a safety hero. Stay curious, stay careful, and stay awesome!"

Chapter 13: Keeping Clean and Healthy

Hi there, Health Hero!

Did you know that keeping your body clean and healthy is one of the best ways to feel great every day? When you wash your hands, brush your teeth, and eat healthy foods, you're giving your body the care it needs to stay strong, energetic, and ready for all your amazing adventures.

In this chapter, we'll discover fun and easy ways to stay clean and healthy. Get ready to become a true Health Hero!

The Healthy Habits Rhyme

"Brush, wash, scrub, and play,

Stay healthy every single day!

Fruits, veggies, and water too,

Health Heroes know what to do!"

What You'll Learn:

1. Why keeping clean is important for staying healthy.

2. Simple habits like washing hands, brushing teeth, and bathing.

3. How healthy foods and exercise help your body grow strong.

Imagine This:

You've just come inside after playing in the yard. Your hands are covered in dirt, and you can't wait to eat a snack. Instead of wiping your hands on your shirt, you head to the sink, scrub with soap and water, and dry them off with a towel.

Now your hands are sparkling clean, and you can enjoy your snack without any worries. That's how a Health Hero takes care of themselves. Great job!

A Story About Staying Clean and Healthy:

Let's meet Jayden!

Jayden was a fun-loving boy who loved snacks, games, and running around outside. But there was one thing Jayden didn't like: brushing his teeth. Every night, his mom would remind him, "Jayden, it's time to brush your teeth," and every night he would groan, "Do I have to?"

One day, Jayden went to the dentist for a check-up. The dentist showed him a big picture of teeth with tiny "sugar bugs" on them. "These sugar bugs love to stick to teeth if they're not brushed," the dentist explained. "And if they stay too long, they can cause cavities."

Jayden's eyes widened. "I don't want sugar bugs on my teeth!"

The dentist smiled. "That's why we brush for two minutes, twice a day. It keeps your teeth clean and strong."

That night, Jayden grabbed his toothbrush without

being asked. He scrubbed for two whole minutes, humming a fun tune while he brushed. "Goodbye, sugar bugs!" he said.

After a week of brushing every morning and night, Jayden's mom noticed something. "Your smile looks extra shiny, Jayden!" she said.

Jayden grinned proudly. He realized that staying clean wasn't just about following rules. It made him feel great too. From that day on, Jayden became a Health Hero, brushing, washing, and taking care of himself like a pro.

Let's Practice Together!

Activity 1: The Handwashing Song

Materials Needed: Soap, water, and a sink.

Instructions:

1. Learn the **5 steps to clean hands**:

   - **Wet your hands** with water.

   - **Add soap** and lather up.

   - **Scrub for 20 seconds** while singing this song to the tune of "Row, Row, Row Your Boat":

"Wash, wash, wash your hands,
Scrub them nice and clean.
Front and back, between your fingers,
Make them sparkle and gleam!"

   - **Rinse** with water.

   - **Dry** your hands with a towel.

2. Practice washing your hands after playing, before eating, and after using the bathroom.

Activity 2: Healthy Habits Chart

Materials Needed: Paper, markers, and stickers or checkmarks.

Instructions:

1. Create a weekly chart with spaces for these healthy habits:
   - Brush teeth twice a day.
   - Wash hands before meals.
   - Eat a fruit or vegetable every day.
   - Drink plenty of water.
   - Get at least 15 minutes of active play (like running or dancing).

2. Each time you complete a habit, add a sticker or draw a smiley face in the box.

3. At the end of the week, celebrate your progress with a family high-five or small reward!

Quick Tips for Staying Healthy:

1. **Brush your teeth** for two minutes in the morning and at night.

2. **Wash your hands** after playing, before eating, and after using the bathroom.

3. Take a **bath or shower** regularly to keep your skin clean.

4. Eat colourful **fruits and veggies** to give your body energy and strength.

5. **Exercise** by running, jumping, or dancing, moving your body is fun and keeps you healthy!

Reflection Time:

- What's one thing you already do to keep your body clean and healthy?

- What's a new healthy habit you can start practicing today?

Superpower Badge: Health Hero

Congratulations! You've earned the Health Hero Badge!
Every time you brush your teeth, wash your hands, or eat something healthy, you're protecting your body and staying strong. Draw a badge with a toothbrush or a piece of fruit to remind yourself that you're a true Health Hero!

Tips for Grown-Ups:

1. **Make It Fun:** Use songs, games, or colourful tools like toothbrushes with fun designs to make hygiene routines exciting.

2. **Set a Routine:** Keep habits consistent, like brushing teeth after breakfast and before bed.

3. **Praise Progress:** Celebrate small wins, like remembering to wash hands without being reminded or eating an extra vegetable at dinner.

- 90 -

Wrap-Up Message:

"Taking care of your body is like giving it a big thank-you for all the amazing things it does for you. When you stay clean, healthy, and active, you're ready for all the fun and adventures life has to offer. Keep it up-you're a Health Hero!"

Conclusion: You're Ready to Shine!

You Did It, Superstar!

Wow, look how much you've learned! From growing a happy mind to staying safe and healthy, you've explored all kinds of cool life skills that will help you every single day. You're like a real-life hero, ready to shine wherever you go!

Let's Celebrate Your Achievements:

- **You can grow a happy and confident mind** by trying your best and never giving up.

- **You know when to speak up and when to stay calm** to help keep yourself and others safe.

- **You respect other people's personal bubbles** and ask before hugging or touching.

- **You've learned the superpower of patience,** waiting your turn even when it's hard.

- **You understand your feelings** and know how to share them with others.

- **You're a pro at sharing, taking turns, and being kind,** making playtime more fun for everyone.

- **You listen carefully and follow instructions** so you can learn, stay safe, and have fun.

- **You speak clearly and kindly**, using your words to spread happiness and understanding.

- **You explore the world around you**, asking big questions and discovering cool new things.

- **You know how to ask for help when you need it**, which makes you strong and smart.

- **You help out at home**, showing your family how much you care.

- **You stay safe and smart** by following important rules wherever you go.

- **You keep clean and healthy**, giving your body the love it deserves.

Look at all these incredible skills you've mastered! You're ready to use them every day to grow, learn, and shine bright like the superstar you are.

What Happens Next?

Now that you've learned these skills, the next step is practicing them. Every time you share, listen, wait, or help, you're becoming even better at being YOU. And remember, it's okay to make mistakes along the way, mistakes are just part of learning.

Here's a little secret: grown-ups are still practicing these skills, too! That's right, even adults are learning how to be more patient, listen better, or ask for help. So, if something feels tricky at first, don't worry. You're already on the right path.

A Special Challenge Just for You

Here's your mission, superstar:

- Pick one skill from this book and practice it today.

- Share something you learned with a friend or family member.

- Celebrate your progress with a happy dance or a high-five, because you're awesome!

Your Grown-Up Helpers

Remember, you have a team of grown-ups in your life who are always here to help you. Whether it's your parents, teachers, or caregivers, they love seeing you grow and are ready to guide you when you need it. Don't be shy about asking for their help, they're your biggest fans!

You're a Superstar!

Every time you try your best, learn something new, or show kindness to others, you're making the world a better place. Keep practicing, exploring, and being the amazing person you are.

The world is so lucky to have someone as awesome as you. So go out there and shine your brightest-you've got this!

One Last Reminder:

"Life is full of adventures, big and small. With the skills you've learned in this book, you're ready to take on anything. So, keep trying, keep shining, and always believe in yourself-you've got this!"

High-five, superstar-you're ready for your next adventure!

Thank you for reading! Reviews are incredibly helpful to authors and other readers. if you enjoyed this book, please consider leaving an honest review. Your feedback helps improve future books and is greatly appreciated!

Apt Lines

9 798230 028437